Excel
Basic Skills

T0342984

English and Mathematics

Year
1
Ages
6-7

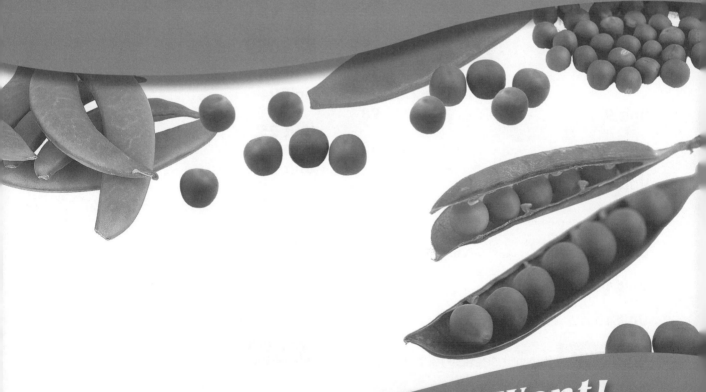

Get the Results You Want!

PASCAL
PRESS

Tanya Dalgleish

Contents

Introduction

The *Excel* Basic Skills Workbook series aims to build and reinforce basic skills in reading, comprehension and mathematics.

The series has eight English and Mathematics core books, one for each of the school years Kindergarten/Foundation to Year 7. These are supported by teaching books, which can be used if the student needs help in a particular area of study.

The structure of this book

This book has 30 carefully sequenced double-page units. Each unit has work on Number, Measurement and Geometry in Maths, and Reading and Comprehension, Spelling and Vocabulary, and Grammar and Punctuation in English.

The student's competence in each of the 30 units can be recorded on the marking grid on pages 5 and 7. There are four end-of-term reviews. These are referred to as Tests 1 to 4. They assess the student's understanding of work covered during each term.

How to use this book

It is recommended that students complete each unit in the sequence provided because the knowledge and understanding developed in each unit is consolidated and practised in subsequent units. The workbook can be used to cover core classroom work. It can also be used to provide homework and consolidation activities.

All units are written so that particular questions deal with the same areas of learning in each unit. For example, question 1 is always on Number (addition) and question 5 is always on Fractions, and so on. Similarly in the English units question 1 is always on Reading and Comprehension, and question 11 is always on Punctuation. Question formatting is repeated throughout the workbook to support familiarity so that students can more readily deal with the Mathematics and English content.

The marking grids (see the examples on pages 4 and 6) are easy-to-use tools for recording students' progress. If you find that certain questions are repeatedly causing difficulties and errors, then there is a specific *Excel* Basic/Advanced Skills Workbook to help students fully revise that topic.

These are the teaching books of the series; they will take students through the topic step by step. The use of illustrations and diagrams, practice questions, and a straightforward and simple approach will make some of the most common problem areas of English and Mathematics easy to understand and master.

Sample Maths Marking Grid

If a student is consistently getting more than **one in five** questions wrong in any area, refer to the highlighted *Excel* Basic Skills title. When marking answers on the grid, simply mark incorrect answers with 'X' in the appropriate box. This will result in a graphical representation of areas needing further work. An example has been done below for the first seven units. If a question has several parts, it should be counted as wrong if one or more mistakes are made.

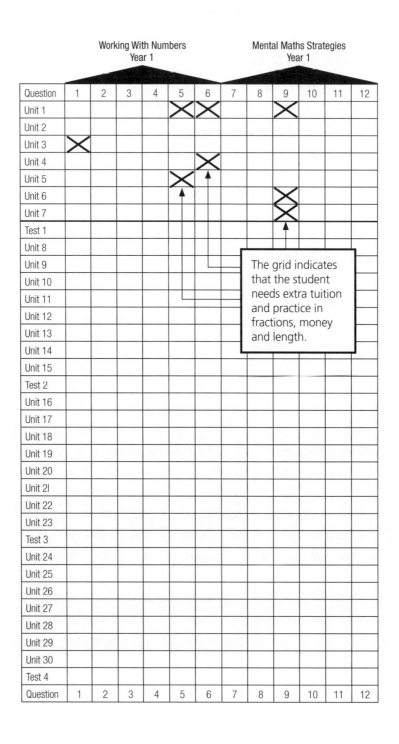

The grid indicates that the student needs extra tuition and practice in fractions, money and length.

Maths Marking Grid

Question	Addition	Subtraction	Counting Numbers	Writing Numbers	Fractions	Money	Time	Mass and Area	Length	Volume	Shapes and Patterns	Position
	1	2	3	4	5	6	7	8	9	10	11	12
Unit 1												
Unit 2												
Unit 3												
Unit 4												
Unit 5												
Unit 6												
Unit 7												
Test 1												
Unit 8												
Unit 9												
Unit 10												
Unit 11												
Unit 12												
Unit 13												
Unit 14												
Unit 15												
Test 2												
Unit 16												
Unit 17												
Unit 18												
Unit 19												
Unit 20												
Unit 2I												
Unit 22												
Unit 23												
Test 3												
Unit 24												
Unit 25												
Unit 26												
Unit 27												
Unit 28												
Unit 29												
Unit 30												
Test 4												
Question	1	2	3	4	5	6	7	8	9	10	11	12

If a student is consistently getting more than **one in five** questions wrong in any area, refer to the highlighted *Excel* Advanced Skills title. When marking answers on the grid, simply mark incorrect answers with 'X' in the appropriate box. This will result in a graphical representation of areas needing further work. An example has been done below for the first seven units.

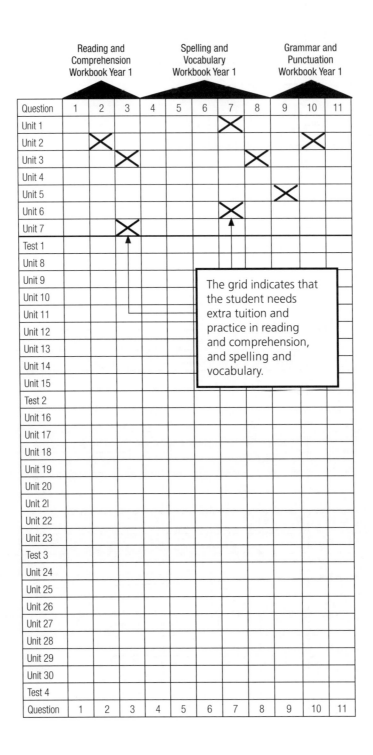

The grid indicates that the student needs extra tuition and practice in reading and comprehension, and spelling and vocabulary.

English Marking Grid

Question	Reading and Comprehension			Spelling and Vocabulary					Grammar and Punctuation		
	1	2	3	4	5	6	7	8	9	10	11
Unit 1											
Unit 2											
Unit 3											
Unit 4											
Unit 5											
Unit 6											
Unit 7											
Test 1											
Unit 8											
Unit 9											
Unit 10											
Unit 11											
Unit 12											
Unit 13											
Unit 14											
Unit 15											
Test 2											
Unit 16											
Unit 17											
Unit 18											
Unit 19											
Unit 20											
Unit 21											
Unit 22											
Unit 23											
Test 3											
Unit 24											
Unit 25											
Unit 26											
Unit 27											
Unit 28											
Unit 29											
Unit 30											
Test 4											
Question	1	2	3	4	5	6	7	8	9	10	11

Mathematics

NUMBER

1

Add 1 more fish to the tank.

How many fish? ☐

2

The bird ate 1 worm. How many are left? ☐

3

How many?

● ☐
● ☐
●

● ● ● ☐
● ● ● ☐

4

Write the words.

1 _____   **2** _____

5

Colour one half.

6

Link: 5c

10c

20c

MEASUREMENT

7

The day after Monday is

_____ .

8

Circle the open shape.

9

Circle the longer object.

10

Colour the jug which is full.

GEOMETRY

11

Trace the circle.

12

Draw a bee **on** the flower.

I went to the shop to get food for my pets.

They like dry food best.

1   READING & COMPREHENSION

Circle the correct word from the text.

I went to a (shop / school / park / movie).

2

They (have / shop / like / pets) dry food best.

3

I went to get _____ .

4   SPELLING & VOCABULARY   **5**

Spell these words from the text.

___ e t

s h o ___

Molly's Pets

NOW OPEN

6   **7**

p ___ t s

Make rhyming words.   pet

m ___ t   g ___ t

n ___ t   j ___ t

8

Write the plural.   one pet,   two _____

9   GRAMMAR & PUNCTUATION

Nouns are naming words.   Choose a noun from the list.

I have a dog, a fish, a rabbit and a _____ .

cat
zebra
car

10

Verbs are action words.   Complete the sentence with a verb.

The cat can _____ .

11

A sentence begins with a capital letter and ends with a full stop.
Write this sentence correctly.

the dog was happy _____

1   NUMBER

 and makes ☐

● and ●●●● makes ☐

2 The girl ate 4 strawberries. Cross them out.

How many are left?

3 Circle the animal which came first in the race.

4 Write the numerals.

one _____

two _____

5 Colour one half.

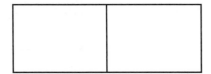

6 Link:

5c	twenty cents
10c	five cents
20c	ten cents

7   MEASUREMENT

The day before Sunday is

_____ .

8 Colour the closed shapes.

9 Draw something wider.

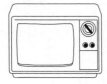

10 Colour to show each container full.

11 Trace and draw a triangle.   GEOMETRY

12 Draw a cat on the mat.

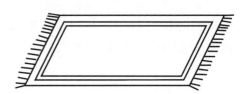

Last Monday I took my cat to the vet because it was sick. The vet gave her a needle.

1

Circle the correct word from the text.

I took my cat to the (park / shop / vet / movies).

2

The vet gave my cat a (drink / needle / tablet / hug).

3

My cat was _____ .

4

Spell these words from the text.

___ a t

5

v e ___

6

c ___ t

7

Make rhyming words. cat

s ___ t   f ___ t

m ___ t   h ___ t

8

Write the plural. one cat, two _____

9

Nouns are naming words. Choose a noun from the list.

A _____ helps sick pets.

vet
doctor
dentist

10

Verbs are action words. Circle the verb.

The cat can catch a mouse.

11

A sentence begins with a capital letter and ends with a full stop.
Write this sentence correctly.

the cat was sick _____

NUMBER

1

Add 3 more apples. How many?

2

Take off 3 apples. How many are left?

3

Draw 3 fish.

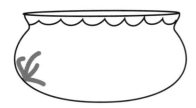

4

Write the words.

3 _____

4 _____

5

Draw the other half.

6

Number the coins in order of value from least to most.

____   ____   ____

MEASUREMENT

7

Circle the daytime activity.

8

Colour the lighter animal.

9

Draw a shorter line.

_____

10

Link.

empty

full

GEOMETRY

11

Colour the triangles blue.

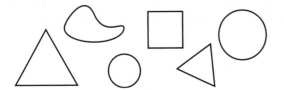

12

Draw a rat on the hat.

English

 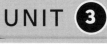

On Sunday my mum and I made a new kennel for my dog, Sam. We made it out of wood.

---

1 Circle the correct word. READING & COMPREHENSION

I made a kennel for my (cat / rabbit / dog / mouse).

2 I made the kennel with my (dad / sister / nanna / mum).

3 The kennel was made of _____ .

---

4 SPELLING & VOCABULARY **5**

Spell these words from the text.

___ a m

d o ___

6 **7**

M ___ m

Make rhyming words. dog

h ___ ___   f ___ ___

f r ___ ___   l ___ ___

---

8 Write the plural. one dog, two _____

---

9 GRAMMAR & PUNCTUATION

Nouns are naming words.
Link the labels to the correct body parts.

head   tail

nose   leg

10 Verbs are action words. Complete the sentence with a verb.

The dog can _____ .

11 A sentence begins with a capital letter and ends with a full stop.
Unscramble the words and write the sentence correctly.

dog my has new kennel a _____

Mathematics

1 NUMBER

●●● and ●●● makes ☐

●● and ●● makes ☐

2 Four bees. Two flew away.
Draw how many are left.

3 Link the numeral with the dots.

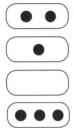

0
3
1
2

4 Write the numerals.

three _____   four _____

five _____

5 Chop the apple in half.

6 Number the coins in order of value from least to most.

_____ _____ _____

7 MEASUREMENT Circle the nighttime activity.

8 Draw bananas to balance the scale.

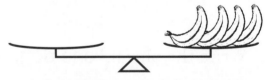

9 Colour the shorter one.

10 Tick which holds more.

11 GEOMETRY Complete the pattern.

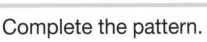

 _____

12 Draw a fish above the tank.

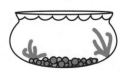

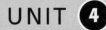

The little monster was sad because he had no friends. The little girl went to play with him. They played hide and seek.

1   READING & COMPREHENSION

Circle the correct word from the text.

The little monster was (happy / sad / hungry / tired).

2

The monster played with the little (boy / girl / dog / rabbit).

3

The monster and the girl played _____ .

4   SPELLING & VOCABULARY   **5**

Spell these words from the text.

___ a d

g i r ___

6   **7**

m ___ n s t e r

Make rhyming words. sad

m ___ ___   b ___ ___

D ___ ___   g l ___ ___

8

Write the plural. one monster, two _____

9   GRAMMAR & PUNCTUATION

Nouns are naming words. Circle the nouns.

monster   girl   play   sad

10

Verbs are action words. Complete the sentence with a verb.

The little monster _____ games.

11

A sentence begins with a capital letter and ends with a full stop.
Write the sentence correctly.   the little girl hid from the monster

_____

Mathematics

NUMBER

1 How many legs?

2 + 2 = ☐

2 5 eggs. 2 broke.

How many are left? ☐

3 Colour 3 fish.

4 Write in words.

5 _____

6 _____

5 Colour half the sweets.

6 Write the words.

50c _____

MEASUREMENT

7 Number the events
1, 2, 3 in the order they occur.

___ playing
___ sleeping
___ going to school

8 Colour the closed shapes.

9 Colour the tallest child.

10 Circle which holds less.

GEOMETRY

11 Colour the squares red.

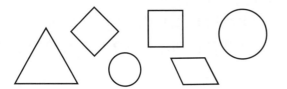

12 The flower is (beside / on / in) the tree.

16

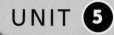
At night the toys in the toy box play games. The tin soldier dances with the ballerina and the Jack-in-the-Box jumps out of his box.

1 READING & COMPREHENSION

Circle the correct word from the text.

The tin soldier dances with the (Jack-in-the-Box / ballerina / boxer).

2

The Jack-in-the-Box (hides / yells / jumps / dances).

3

The toys play _____ .

4 SPELLING & VOCABULARY **5**

Spell these words from the text.

t i ___

___ o x

6 **7**

t ___ n

Make rhyming words. tin

b ____ ____   p ____ ____

f ____ ____   s h ____ ____

8

Write the plural. one toy, two _____

9 GRAMMAR & PUNCTUATION

Nouns are naming words. Choose a noun from the list.

The toys are kept in a _____ .

cupboard
crate
box

10

Verbs are action words. Complete the sentence with a verb.

The tin soldier and ballerina _____ .

11

A sentence begins with a capital letter and ends with a full stop. Write the sentence correctly.

the toys play games _____

NUMBER

1

$1 + 4 =$ ☐

2

Cross out 3.
How many are left? ☐

3

Colour the animal which came second in the race.

4

Write the numerals.

five _____

six _____

5

Colour half the teddy.

6

Match.

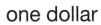 one dollar

 fifty cents

MEASUREMENT

7

Tick the activity which takes longer.

eating breakfast ___

jumping 10 jumps ___

8

Circle the heavier animal.

9

Draw a thicker snake.

10

Circle the containers that will hold water.

GEOMETRY

11

Colour the diamond green.

12

Colour the ball on the right.

The little lost kitten found a good home with the two children, Jenny and Jeff.
They called the kitten Fluff Puff.

1   READING & COMPREHENSION

Circle the correct word from the text.

The kitten's name was (Puff Fluff / Jenny / Jeff / Fluff Puff).

2

The kitten was (sad / hungry / lost / lonely).

3

The kitten found a good _____ .

4   SPELLING & VOCABULARY   **5**

Spell these words from the text.

___ i t t e n

l o s ___

6   **7**

f l ___ f f

Make rhyming words.

fluff   h _____

p _____   s t _____

8

Write the plural. one kitten, two _____

9   GRAMMAR & PUNCTUATION

People's names are proper nouns. Choose a proper noun from the list. _____ patted the kitten.

> Jeff, dog, cat, children

10

Verbs are action words. Complete the sentence with a verb.

Kittens can _____ .

11

A sentence begins with a capital letter and ends with a full stop.
Write the sentence correctly.   the children found a lost kitten

_____

Mathematics

NUMBER

1

 +

$2 + 3 =$ ☐

2

Cross out 2.

How many are left? ☐

3

Colour the animal which came third in the race.

4

Write the words.

7 _____

8 _____

5

Colour the things that are cut in half.

6

Match.

10c   20c   50c $1

MEASUREMENT

7

Circle the activity which takes the shorter time.

Having a bath.

Clapping hands 10 times.

8

The bicycle is (lighter / heavier) than the truck.

9

Tick the longest line.

_____

_____

_____

10

Circle those which will hold beads.

GEOMETRY

11

Link:

circle   ☐

triangle   ○

square   △

12

Help the baby find its mother.

20

The three Billy Goats Gruff ran across the bridge. They were glad to be safe from the Troll who lived under the bridge.

1 READING & COMPREHENSION

Circle the correct word from the text.

A Troll lived under the (road / bridge / building / tree).

2

The Billy Goats were glad to be (safe / running / hungry / lonely).

3

There were _____ Billy Goats Gruff.

4 SPELLING & VOCABULARY **5**

Spell these words from the text.

f r o___

g l a ___

6 **7**

r ___ n

Make rhyming words.

glad   m _____

b _____   s _____

8

Write the plural. one goat, two _____

9 GRAMMAR & PUNCTUATION

Nouns are naming words. Choose a noun from the list.

The goats ran across the _____ .

bridge, river, road, safe

10

Verbs are action words. Complete the sentence with a verb.

The Billy Goats _____ .

11

A sentence begins with a capital letter and ends with a full stop. Write the sentence correctly.

trolls eat goats _____

21

1   NUMBER

 = ⬜

 = ⬜

2

6 ice creams were eaten.

How many are left?

3

Circle the animal which came third in the race.

4

Write the words.

1 _____

2 _____

3 _____

5

Colour half the fish.

6

Number the coins in order from least to most.

_____   _____   _____

_____   _____   _____

7

MEASUREMENT

Name something
you do in the morning.

_____

Name something you do in the
afternoon.

_____

8

Draw pineapples to
balance the scale.

9

Draw a cat with a longer tail.

10

Circle the jug which is full.

11

GEOMETRY

Colour the circle red and
the square blue.

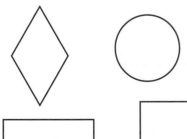

12

Circle the bird above the
tree and colour the cat
on the right of the tree.

My cat, Fluffy, and my dog, Jack, like to play

together. They like to play hide and seek.

At night they sleep together in a box.

They are good friends.

READING & COMPREHENSION

1

Circle the correct word from the text.

The cat's name is (dog / Fluffy / Jack / friend).

2

The cat and dog are (sleepy / naughty / friends / children).

3

Fluffy and Jack sleep in a _____ .

SPELLING & VOCABULARY

4

Spell these words from the text.

c __ t

5

d __ g

6

g __ __ d

7   Make rhyming words.

cat   p _____   b _____   r _____

play   d _____   s t _____   m _____

8   Write the plurals.

cat _____

friend _____   dog _____

9   GRAMMAR & PUNCTUATION

Complete with a proper noun from the box.

_____ and Jack are good friends.

| dogs |
| cats |
| box |
| Fluffy |

10   Complete the sentence with a verb.

Fluffy and Jack _____ games.

11   Write the sentence correctly.

the dog and cat are friends

_____

1   NUMBER

✏️✏️ + ✏️✏️✏️✏️ = ☐

2 + 4 = ☐

2

There were 8 birds.
4 flew away.

How many are left? ☐

3   Complete each row.

7 🐟 🐟

4 🐟 🐟

4

Write in numerals.

seven _____

eight _____

5   Put half the apples in each jar.

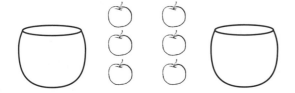

6   Circle which costs more.

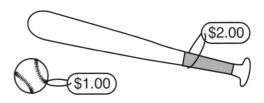

$2.00

$1.00

7   MEASUREMENT

Number the months in order.

January	___	April	___
February	___	May	___
March	___	June	___

8

The pineapple is
(heavier / lighter) than the apple.

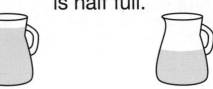

9   Number in order from
shortest to longest.

—————   ——

———————   ——

————————   ——

10

Circle the jug which
is half full.

11   GEOMETRY

How many
rectangles?

_____

12

The cat is
(on / under / beside) the table.

Ants are insects.

They have six legs and three body parts.

Ants live in colonies with other ants.

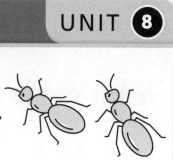

1

READING & COMPREHENSION

Circle the correct word from the text.

Ants are (mammals, insects, birds, fish).

2

Ants have six (eyes, feet, legs, ants).

3

Ants live with other _____ .

4

SPELLING & VOCABULARY

Spell these words from the text.

l e ___

5

___ o d y

6

___ n t

7

Make rhyming words.

ants   p _____

pl _____   ch _____

8

Write the plural.   one ant, two _____

9

GRAMMAR & PUNCTUATION

Nouns are naming words. Choose a noun from the box.

All _____ have six legs.

> dogs, cats, boys, insects

10

Verbs are action words. Complete the sentence with a verb.

Sometimes ants _____ people.

11

A sentence begins with a capital letter and ends with a full stop.
Write this sentence correctly.

ants have six legs _____

Mathematics

1
NUMBER

 + 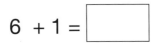 = ☐

6 + 1 = ☐

2

Lose 4 marbles.

How many are left?

3

Colour the tree with zero apples.

4

Write in numerals.

five _____   seven _____

six _____   eight _____

5

Colour one half of the apple.

6

Write the numbers on the coins.

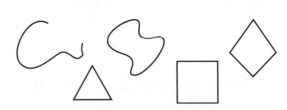

7
MEASUREMENT

Circle the school days.

Monday   Tuesday   Wednesday

Thursday   Friday   Saturday

Sunday

8

Circle the open shapes.

9

Draw something narrower.

10

Circle the things that would fit in the box.

11
GEOMETRY

Name the shape.

_____

12

The dog is (inside / outside) the kennel.

28

Spiders are not insects.
Spiders have eight legs.
Some spiders build webs to catch their food.

1   READING & COMPREHENSION

Circle the correct word from the text.

Spiders are not (small / insects / webs / dogs).

2

Spiders have eight (heads / legs / eyes / fangs).

3

Some spiders build _____ .

4   SPELLING & VOCABULARY   **5**

Spell these words from the text.

___ o o d

n o ___

6   **7**

w e ___

Make rhyming words.

leg   p _____

b _____   M _____

8

Write the plural.   one leg, eight _____

9   GRAMMAR & PUNCTUATION

Nouns are naming words. Circle the nouns.

spider   legs   catch   food

10

Verbs are action words. Choose a verb from the list.

Some spiders _____ webs.

catch, spider, build, webs

11

A sentence begins with a capital letter and ends with a full stop. Write this sentence correctly.

spiders have eight legs _____

1
NUMBER

☆☆☆☆☆☆ + ☆☆☆☆ = ☐

6 + 4 = ☐

2

3 balloons burst.

How many are left? ☐

3

Write the missing numbers.

_____ , 1, 2, 3, _____ , 5

4

Write in words.

9 _____

10 _____

5

Colour half of each shape.

6

Circle which coin is wrong.

7
MEASUREMENT

Write something that takes more time than writing your name.

_____

8

Draw a bigger dog.

9

The pencil is (longer / shorter) than the belt.

10

Circle the jug which has more water in it.

11
GEOMETRY

Name the shape.

_____

12

The beetle is (under / over) the leaf.

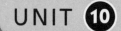

Crocodiles are reptiles.

They live in rivers in hot countries.

They have sharp teeth and are dangerous.

---

1   READING & COMPREHENSION

Circle the correct word from the text.

Crocodiles are (teeth / insects / dangerous / rivers).

2

Crocodiles have sharp (feet / nostrils / teeth / eyes).

3

Crocodiles are r _____ .

---

4   SPELLING & VOCABULARY   **5**

Spell these words from the text.

___ e e t h

s h a r ___

---

6   **7**

l i v ___

Make rhyming words.

hot   p _____

n _____   sl _____

8

Write the plural.   one crocodile, two _____

---

9   GRAMMAR & PUNCTUATION

Nouns are naming words.

Link the labels to the crocodile.   leg

tail   teeth

head

10

Verbs are action words. Circle the verbs that describe what a crocodile can do.

swim   fly   eat   bite

11

A sentence begins with a capital letter and ends with a full stop.
Write this sentence correctly.   crocodiles have sharp teeth

_____

1 NUMBER

 + 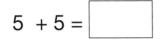 = [ ]

5 + 5 = [ ]

2

Eat 3 cakes.

How many are left? [ ]

3 Join the dots.

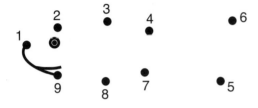

4 Write the numerals.

nine _____

ten _____

5 Colour half of each shape.

6 Link.

$1.00 $2.00   50c

7 MEASUREMENT

What day comes after
Wednesday?

_____

8 Draw a closed shape.

9 The snake is
(longer / shorter) than the worm.

10 Circle the container that
holds the most.

11 GEOMETRY

How many triangles? [ ]

12 Which cat will catch the
mouse? Trace the path.

People need exercise.
We need to hop, jump, skip, run, play
sport or walk every day to stay healthy.

---

1   READING & COMPREHENSION

Circle the correct word from the text.

People need exercise every (week / day / month / night).

2

Walking is good _____ .

3

Exercise keeps us _____ .

4   SPELLING & VOCABULARY   **5**

Spell these words from the text.

____ o p

j u m ____

6   Make rhyming words. **7**

r ____ n

hop   p _____

pl _____   st _____

8

Write the plural. **one person, many** _____

9   GRAMMAR & PUNCTUATION

Nouns are naming words. Choose a noun from the list.

People need to exercise every _____ .

> night, day,
> morning,
> year

10

Verbs are action words. Circle the verbs.

hop skip jump people walk run day

11

A sentence begins with a capital letter and ends with a full stop.
Write this sentence correctly. exercise is good for you

_____

Mathematics

NUMBER

1

✓✓✓✓ + ✓✓✓✓ = ☐

5 + 4 = ☐

2

6 birds flew away.

How many are left? ☐

3

Join the dots.

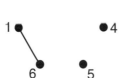

2   3

1   •4

6   •5

4

Write the missing numbers on the number line.

1   4 5 6   10

5

Colour half of each shape.

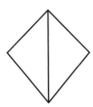

6

Circle the coin which is not Australian.

MEASUREMENT

7

Draw something you do at night.

8

Draw an open shape.

9

Draw something that is the same length as your foot.

10

Colour the jug to show that it is full.

GEOMETRY

11

Colour the diamonds.

12

Which bird will get the worm?

34

My friend's name is Lan. Lan was born in Hong Kong. Hong Kong is in China. Lan's name means 'orchid' in Chinese.

1   READING & COMPREHENSION

Circle the correct word from the text.

Hong Kong is in (Australia / China / Japan).

2

Lan's name means ('hello' / 'orchid' / 'orchard').

3

Lan is _____ .

4   SPELLING & VOCABULARY   **5**

Spell these words from the text.

C h ___ n a

n ___ m e

6   **7**

f r ___ e n d

Make rhyming words. name

f _____   g _____

t _____   l _____

8

Write the plural.   one child, many _____

9   GRAMMAR & PUNCTUATION

Adjectives are describing words. Choose an adjective from the list.

Lan is a _____ friend.

> good, bad, hot, cold

10

Verbs are action words. Complete the sentence with a verb.

I like to _____ with Lan.

11

A question begins with a capital letter and ends with a question mark. Write this question correctly.

where was Lan born _____

Mathematics

1

NUMBER

✻ ✻ ✻ ✻ ✻ + ✻
✻ ✻ ✻ ✻

9 + 1 = ☐

2

10 oranges. 1 was eaten.
Draw how many are left.

3

What number comes
before 5?

_____

4

Complete.

1, 2, 3, _____ ,

5, _____ , 7, 8

5

Colour half of the
balloons blue.

6

Circle the Australian coin.

7

MEASUREMENT

Draw something
you do in the
daytime.

8

The apple is

_____

than the dog.
(heavier / lighter)

9

Draw something that is
shorter than your thumb.

10

Circle the things that would
not fit in a box.

11

GEOMETRY

Complete the pattern.

 ___ ___

12

Draw a girl
up and a
boy down.

Monsoon season is the wet season in Kakadu. There are thunderstorms which bring heavy rain. Monsoon season is very hot.

1   READING & COMPREHENSION

Circle the correct word from the text.

Monsoon season in Kakadu is (cold / wet / dry / snowy).

2   Monsoon season is also called the (wet / dry / autumn / spring) season.

3   Thunderstorms can bring _____ .

4   SPELLING & VOCABULARY   **5**

Spell these words from the text.

w ___ t

h ___ t

6

r ___ i n

7 Make rhyming words

bring   t h _____

f l _____   str _____

8   Write the plural.   one storm, many _____

9   GRAMMAR & PUNCTUATION

Names of particular places are proper nouns.
Write the name of the place in the text.

_____

10   Adjectives are describing words. Circle the adjectives.

hot   wet   rainy   storm   rain   cloudy   thunder   Kakadu

11   Proper nouns start with a capital letter.
Write the sentence correctly.   in kakadu there are six seasons

_____

Mathematics

NUMBER

1

✳✳ + ✳✳✳✳✳
✳✳✳✳

2 + 9 = ☐

2

5 flew away.

How many are left? ☐

3

What number comes
after 9?

_____

4

Write in words.

10 _____

11 _____

5

Colour one half
of the elephant.

6

Circle the coin needed
to buy the comb.

$2.00

MEASUREMENT

7

How many
months are in 1 year?_____

How many
days are in 1 week?_____

8

Draw something
that has nearly
the same mass
as an apple.

9

Circle the tallest tree.

10

Which holds the most water?
Circle it.

GEOMETRY

11

Use the shapes
to draw a car.

  ◯

12

Colour blue
the fish on
the left.

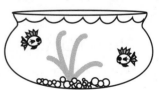

Auslan is a sign language for Australians. Auslan uses hand shapes and movement. Learning Auslan is fun. I like the Auslan sign (symbol) for helicopter.

1   READING & COMPREHENSION

Circle the correct word from the text.

Auslan is a (helicopter / hand / symbol / language).

2

Auslan is _____ to learn.

3

Auslan uses _____ shapes and movement.

4   SPELLING & VOCABULARY   **5**

Spell these words from the text.

s i ___ n

I ___ k e

6

u s ___ s

7 Make rhyming words.

hand   b _____

l _____   st _____

8 Write the plural.   one shape, two _____

9   GRAMMAR & PUNCTUATION

Nouns are naming words. Choose a noun from the box.

We use our _____ to communicate in Auslan.

| helicopters hands feet snakes |

10 Proper nouns start with a capital letter. Write two proper nouns from the text.

_____   _____

11 A question begins with a capital letter and ends with a question mark. Write this question correctly.   would you like to learn Auslan

_____

1   NUMBER

 + = ☐

$12 + 0 =$ ☐

2

10 take away 3 equals ☐

3

____ , 5, 4, 3, 2, 1, 0

4

Write the numerals.

ten ____   twelve ____

eleven ____   thirteen ____

5

Colour half.

6

 = ☐

7   MEASUREMENT

What month is your birthday?

_____

8

Colour the shape with the smaller area.

9   Trace the shorter path.

10

11   GEOMETRY

Draw the other half.

12

Colour red the dragon on top.

Some of the oldest paintings in the world can be found on rocks and in caves in remote parts of Australia.

1   READING & COMPREHENSION

Circle the correct word from the text.

The paintings are on (cars / boats / rocks / trees).

2

The paintings are (new / caves / found / old).

3

Some paintings are in _____ .

4   SPELLING & VOCABULARY   **5**

Spell these words from the text.

r ___ c k s

c ___ v e s

6

s ___ m e

7

Make rhyming words.

found   s _____

h _____   gr _____

8

Write the plural.   one rock, three _____

9   GRAMMAR & PUNCTUATION

Names of particular places are proper nouns. They start with a capital letter. Write the proper noun from the text.

_____

10

Adjectives are describing words. Choose an adjective from the box.

The rock paintings are very _____.

wet, old, fluffy, soft

11

A question begins with a capital letter and ends with a question mark. Write this question correctly.

how old are the paintings _____

Mathematics

1

NUMBER

✖✖✖✖   ✖✖✖✖✖

4   +   5   =   ☐

✔✔✔✔✔   ✔✔✔
✔✔✔✔✔

10   +   3   =   ☐

2

10 pencils. 8 were sold.

How many are left?   ☐

3

Join the dots.

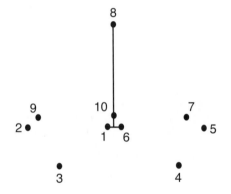

4

Fill in the missing numbers.

0, ____ , ____ ,

3, 4, ____ ,

6, ____ , 8, 9, ____

5

Colour one half
of each shape.

6

Circle the animal which
belongs on the coin.

20

Answers

UNIT ① page 8

Maths
1. 3
2. 2
3. (reading L to R) 2 , 6, 1, 0
4. one, two
5. Either side is half.
6. Parent/teacher to check.
7. Tuesday
8. The line on the left is open.
9. The pencil is longer.
10. Colour the jug on the left.
11. Parent/teacher to check.
12. Parent/teacher to check.

English
1. shop
2. like
3. food
4. get
5. shop
6. pets
7. met get net jet
8. pets
9. cat
10. Answers will vary.
11. The dog was happy.

UNIT ② page 10

Maths
1. 3 dots or 3, 5 dots or 5
2. 2
3. zebra
4. 1, 2
5. Either side is half.
6. 5c—five cents; 10c—ten cents; 20c—twenty cents
7. Saturday
8. Colour the triangle and the circle.
9. Parent/teacher to check.
10. Parent/teacher to check.
11. Parent/teacher to check.
12. Parent/teacher to check.

English
1. vet
2. needle
3. sick
4. cat
5. vet
6. cat
7. sat fat mat hat
8. cats
9. vet
10. catch
11. The cat was sick.

UNIT ③ page 12

Maths
1. 5
2. 1
3. Parent/teacher to check.
4. three, four
5.
6. 3, 1, 2
7. skipping
8. Colour the bird.
9. Parent/teacher to check.
10. The top bowl is full, the bottom one empty.
11.
12. Parent/teacher to check.

English
1. dog
2. Mum
3. wood
4. Sam
5. dog
6. Mum
7. hog fog frog log
8. dogs
9.
   head   tail
   nose   leg
10. catch
11. My dog has a new kennel.

UNIT ④ page 14

Maths
1. 6, 4
2. 2 bees
3. Parent/teacher to check.
4. 3, 4, 5
5.
6. 1, 3, 2
7. the person asleep in bed
8. 4 bananas will balance the scale.
9. The kangaroo is shorter.
10. The milk carton holds more.
11. Draw a circle next.
12. Parent/teacher to check.

English
1. sad
2. girl
3. hide and seek
4. sad
5. girl
6. monster
7. mad bad Dad glad
8. monsters
9. monster, girl
10. The little monster played / liked games.
11. The little girl hid from the monster.

UNIT ⑤ page 16

Maths
1. 4
2. 3
3. Parent/teacher to check.
4. five, six
5. 2 sweets
6. fifty cents

Answers

7. 2, 3, 1 or 1, 3, 2
8. Parent/teacher to check.
9. the child on the right
10. The tea cup holds less.
11.
12. beside

English
1. ballerina
2. jumps
3. games
4. tin
5. box
6. tin
7. bin pin fin shin
8. toys
9. box
10. dance
11. The toys play games.

UNIT 6 page 18

Maths
1. 5
2. 2
3. the hippo
4. 5, 6
5.
6. Fifty cents is the top coin, one dollar is the bottom coin.
7. Parent/teacher to check.
8. the elephant
9. Parent/teacher to check.
10. bucket, drink can, tea cup
11. ◇ ○ □ △
12. Parent/teacher to check.

English
1. Fluff Puff
2. lost
3. home
4. kitten
5. lost
6. fluff
7. huff, puff, stuff

8. kittens
9. Jeff
10. Answers will vary.
11. The children found a lost kitten.

UNIT 7 page 20

Maths
1. 5
2. 2
3. pig
4. seven, eight
5. the first circle and the triangle
6. Parent/teacher to check.
7. clapping hands 10 times
8. lighter
9. The bottom line is longest.
10. saucepan and mug
11. The top shape is the square, then the circle and the triangle.
12. Parent/teacher to check.

English
1. bridge
2. safe
3. three
4. from
5. glad
6. ran
7. mad, bad, sad
8. goats
9. The goats ran across the bridge.
10. Answers will vary.
11. Trolls eat goats.

TEST 1 page 22

Maths
1. 7, 5
2. 0
3. snail
4. one, two, three
5. Colour three fish.
6. 5, 6, 2, 3, 4, 1
7. Parent/teacher to check.
8. Draw 4 pineapples.

9. Parent/teacher to check.
10. the jug on the left
11. Parent/teacher to check.
12. Parent/teacher to check.

English
1. Fluffy
2. friends
3. box
4. cat
5. dog
6. good
7. pat, bat, rat
8. cats, friends, dogs
9. Fluffy
10. play
11. The dog and cat are friends.

UNIT 8 page 26

Maths
1. 6, 6
2. 4
3.
4. 7, 8
5. 3 apples in each jar
6. The bat costs more.
7. 1—January, 2—February, 3—March, 4—April, 5—May, 6—June
8. heavier
9. 1, 2, 3
10. the jug on the right
11. 6
12. on

English
1. insects
2. legs
3. ants
4. leg
5. body
6. ant
7. pants, plants, chants
8. ants
9. insects
10. bite
11. Ants have six legs.

ANSWERS: *Excel* Basic Skills English and Mathematics Year 1

Answers

UNIT 9 page 28

Maths
1. 7, 7
2. 4
3. the tree on the left
4. 5, 7, 6, 8
5. Parent/teacher to check.
6. 50, 20, 10
7. Monday, Tuesday, Wednesday, Thursday, Friday
8. Circle the wavy line.
9. Parent/teacher to check.
10. Circle teddy, balloon, cat.
11. rectangle
12. outside

English
1. insects
2. legs
3. webs
4. food
5. not
6. web
7. peg, beg, Meg
8. legs
9. spider, legs, food
10. Some spiders build webs.
11. Spiders have eight legs.

UNIT 10 page 30

Maths
1. 10, 10
2. 3
3. 0, 4
4. nine, ten
5. Parent/teacher to check.
6. The coin on the left is wrong.
7. Parent/teacher to check.
8. Parent/teacher to check.
9. shorter
10. the jug on the right
11. square
12. under

English
1. dangerous
2. teeth

3. reptiles
4. teeth
5. sharp
6. live
7. pot, not, slot
8. crocodiles
9.

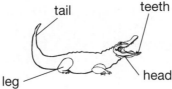

10. swim, eat, bite
11. Crocodiles have sharp teeth.

UNIT 11 page 32

Maths
1. 10, 10
2. 7
3.

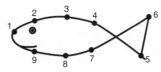

4. 9, 10
5. Parent/teacher to check.
6. The coins are in order (L to R) 50c, $1, $2.
7. Thursday
8. Parent/teacher to check.
9. longer
10. bucket
11. 6
12. Parent/teacher to check.

English
1. day
2. exercise
3. healthy
4. hop
5. jump
6. run
7. pop, plop, stop
8. people
9. day
10. hop, skip, jump, walk, run
11. Exercise is good for you.

UNIT 12 page 34

Maths
1. 9, 9
2. 0
3.

4. 2, 3, 7, 8, 9
5. Parent/teacher to check.
6.

7. Parent/teacher to check.
8. Parent/teacher to check.
9. Parent/teacher to check.
10.

11.

12. the bird closer to the worm

English
1. China
2. orchid
3. Answers will vary.
4. China
5. name
6. friend
7. fame, game, tame, lame
8. children
9. good
10. Answers will vary.
11. Where was Lan born?

UNIT 13 page 36

Maths
1. 10
2. 9
3. 4
4. 4, 6
5. 3 balloons
6.

Answers

7. Parent/teacher to check.
8. lighter
9. Parent/teacher to check.
10. chair, plane, helicopter
11. diamond, triangle
12. Parent/teacher to check.

English
1. wet
2. wet
3. heavy rain/rain
4. wet
5. hot
6. rain
7. thing, fling, string
8. storms
9. Kakadu
10. hot, wet, rainy, cloudy
11. In Kakadu there are six seasons.

UNIT 14 page 38

Maths
1. 11
2. 5
3. 10
4. ten, eleven
5. Parent/teacher to check.
6. Circle $2 coin.
7. 12, 7
8. Parent/teacher to check.
9. tree on left
10. swimming pool
11. Parent/teacher to check.
12. Parent/teacher to check.

English
1. language
2. fun
3. hand
4. sign
5. like
6. uses
7. hand, land, stand
8. shapes
9. hands
10. Auslan, Australians
11. Would you like to learn Auslan?

UNIT 15 page 40

Maths
1. 12, 12
2. 7
3. 6
4. (reading L to R) 10, 12, 11, 13
5.
6. 30c
7. Parent/teacher to check.
8. the 4 square shape on the left
9. The straight line is the shorter path.
10.
11.
12. Parent/teacher to check.

English
1. rocks
2. old
3. caves
4. rocks
5. caves
6. some
7. sound, hound, ground
8. rocks
9. Australia
10. old
11. How old are the paintings?

TEST 2 page 42

Maths
1. 9, 13
2. 2
3.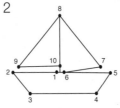

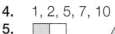
4. 1, 2, 5, 7, 10
5.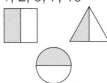
6. platypus
7. Saturday, Sunday
8. the 9 square shape on the right
9. Parent/teacher to check.
10.
11.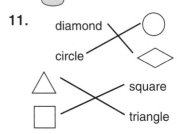
12. Parent/teacher to check.

English
1. mammals
2. pouches
3. milk
4. pouch
5. milk
6. grass
7. sink, stink, pink
   pit, hit, sit
8. kangaroos, mammals, leaves, joeys
9.
10. hot, cold, green, red
11. Kangaroos live in Australia.

UNIT 16 page 46

Maths
1. 20
2. 4
3. Parent/teacher to check.
4. twelve, thirteen, fourteen

5.

6. 60c
7. spring, summer; Parent/ teacher to check.
8. aeroplane
9. middle watch
10.

11. first circle
12. Parent/teacher to check.

English
1. porridge
2. like
3. breakfast
4. Dad
5. warm
6. cooked
7. look, book, took
8. Dads
9. porridge, milk, honey, Dad
10. cooked
11. My sister, Lilly, ate porridge too.

UNIT 17 page 48

Maths
1. 12
2. 4
3. 10
4. fifteen, sixteen, seventeen
5. Parent/teacher to check.
6. $1, 50c
7. beanie, scarf, jacket
8. the 4 square shape
9. the middle watch
10. the jug on the left
11. Parent/teacher to check.
12.

English
1. bus
2. Sunday
3. soup
4. Sunday

---

5. soup
6. day
7. ray, play, stay
8. buses
9. sister, Nanna, Mum
10. ate
11. On Sunday I went to visit Nanna.

UNIT 18 page 50

Maths
1. 17
2. 3
3. 1, 6
4. 18, 19
5.

6. $5, 50c
7. 9 o'clock
8. Parent/teacher to check.
9. bath
10. the smaller teddy on the right
11.

12. Parent/teacher to check.

English
1. park
2. yesterday
3. lunch
4. children
5. lunch
6. picnic
7. punch, munch, crunch
8. lunches
9. lunch
10. played
11. The children had a picnic lunch.

UNIT 19 page 52

Maths
1. 18
2. 10
3. 10

---

4. eighteen, nineteen, twenty
5.

6. $2, 50c
7. The flowers show spring.
8. elephant
9. Parent/teacher to check.
10. The smaller mouse will fit.
11. Row 1: flower, leaf, flower; Row 2: leaf, flower
12.

English
1. today
2. carrot
3. Tran's
4. dear
5. when
6. tooth
7. bake, cake, shake
8. babies
9. tooth, carrot, fairy
10. fell
11. Tran wrote to the Tooth Fairy.

UNIT 20 page 54

Maths
1. 13, 13
2. 14
3. 12
4. 18, 19, 20
5. Colour any 5 bananas.
6. Colour any two 50c pieces.
7. Parent/teacher to check.
8. heavier
9. Parent/teacher to check.
10. Colour the last jug half full.
11. [figure: striped rectangle, triangle, triangle, striped rectangle]

12. Parent/teacher to check.

English
1. mouse
2. ropes
3. free

4. lion
5. net
6. rope
7. beat, meat, treat
8. mice
9. tiger
10. ate / chewed
11. The mouse repaid the lion's kindness.

UNIT 21 page 56

Maths
1. 18
2. 10 − 4 = 6
3. 13
4. 15, 20, 25, 30, 35, 40, 45, 50
5.
6. $1 coin
7. t-shirt , hat
8. Parent/teacher to check.
9. Parent/teacher to check.
10. the two-storey house on the left
11. Parent/teacher to check.
12. bee

English
1. tortoise
2. sleep
3. race
4. hare
5. won
6. race
7. share, fare, dare
8. races
9. tortoise
10. raced
11. Slow and steady wins the race.

UNIT 22 page 58

Maths
1. 15
2. 10 − 5 = 5
3. any combination e.g. 10 + 5; 14 + 1; 12 + 3

4. 10 —— ten
   20 ✕ thirty
   30 ✕ twenty
5. Colour any 9 strawberries.
6. Cross out 2 coins.
7. Parent/teacher to check.
8. 10 spoons are heavier than 6 spoons.
9. The straighter line is shorter.
10. Parent/teacher to check.
11. Parent/teacher to check.
12. Parent/teacher to check.

English
1. legs
2. fly
3. fly
4. very
5. bird
6. fly
7. spy, dry, cry
8. birds
9. bird, emu, eggs
10. fly, walk, eat
11. Emus are Australian birds that cannot fly.

UNIT 23 page 60

Maths
1. 15
2. 10 − 2 = 8
3. 16
4. 40, 60, 50, 70
5.
6. Colour 10 coins.
7. 8 o'clock
8. brick
9. Parent/teacher to check.
10. Colour the jug full.
11.
12. Parent/teacher to check.

English
1. walk

2. car
3. home
4. walk
5. school
6. school
7. hive, five, dive
8. children
9. train
10. Answers will vary
11. Most children at our school come by car.

TEST 3 page 62

Maths
1. 12, 12
2. 15, 12
3. 15
4. 17 ——— 20
   eighteen ✕ nineteen
   19 ——— 18
   twenty seventeen
5. Colour 8 butterflies.
6. Parent/teacher to check.
7. Parent/teacher to check.
8. pineapple
9. The straight line is shorter.
10. The taller flowers suit the vase.
11. Parent/teacher to check.
12. on

English
1. porridge
2. bed
3. chair
4. went
5. chair
6. bear
7. red, led, Ted
   peep, sheep, steep
8. houses, bears, chairs, beds
9. bear, Goldilocks, bed, chair
10. (When Goldilocks saw the bears) She screamed and ran away.
11. Goldilocks went into the house.

Answers

UNIT 24 page 66

Maths

1. 5, 5
2. 10 – 7 = 3
3. 5, 10, 15, 20, 25, 30, 35, 40, 45, 50
4. forty, fifty, sixty
5. Colour 6 red and 6 blue.
6. $2
7. 11 o'clock
8. bee/insect
9. Parent/teacher to check.
10. Parent/teacher to check.
11. Parent/teacher to check.
12. Parent/teacher to check.

English

1. good
2. dirty
3. friendly / clean /interesting
4. clean
5. crab
6. quite
7. mean, bean, lean
8. crabs
9.

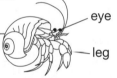

shell — eye

— leg

10. eat, run, crawl, move
11. Hermit crabs eat coconut, bread, biscuits and fish food.

UNIT 25 page 68

Maths

1. 2
2. 12
3. Parent/teacher to check.
4. 70, 80, 90
5.

6. 60c
7. 4 o'clock
8. Any five square shape; Parent/teacher to check.
9. Parent/teacher to check.
10. Parent/teacher to check.

11.

12. Parent/teacher to check.

English

1. fossils
2. meat
3. extinct
4. dinosaur
5. fossil
6. study
7. heat, treat, seat
8. dinosaurs
9. eyes

head

mouth   body

10. run, eat, scratch
11. Dinosaurs are extinct.

UNIT 26 page 70

Maths

1. 12
2. 16
3. Parent/teacher to check.
4. 70 —— seventy
   80 ⤬ ninety
   90 —— eighty
5. Colour any 5 balloons.
6. Colour 5 coins.
7. 5 o'clock
8. Parent/teacher to check.
9. Parent/teacher to check.
10. bucket and tea cup
11.

12. Parent/teacher to check.

English

1. mammals
2. pods
3. milk
4. young
5. mammal
6. whale
7. pale, male, sale
8. mothers
9. mammals
10. feed / give
11. I love whales and dolphins.

UNIT 27 page 72

Maths

1. 13, 15
2. 15, 14
3. The bottom row has more flowers.
4. 100, 90, 80
5. Colour any 6 apples.
6. Least value to most value: 2, 3, 1, 4. Most value to least value: 3, 2, 4, 1
7. 4 o'clock
8. Parent/teacher to check.
9. Parent/teacher to check.
10. bath
11.

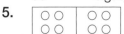

3 2 1   3 2 1   3 2 1

12. Parent/teacher to check.

English

1. night
2. then
3. radio
4. boy
5. when
6. was
7. right, sight, fright
8. families
9. terrific
10. yelled
11. Turn it off!

UNIT 28 page 74

Maths

1. 18, 18
2. 10, 5
3. Parent/teacher to check.
4. 100 ⤬ ninety
   90 ⤬ one hundred
   80 —— eighty
5.

6. $2
7. 3 o'clock
8. Parent/teacher to check.
9. Parent/teacher to check.
10.

11. Parent/teacher to check.
12.

English
1. teeth
2. day
3. calcium
4. food
5. teeth
6. how
7. cow, now, sow
8. teeth
9. yoghurt, milk, apples, cheese
10. clean / brush
11. Brush your teeth before you go to bed.

UNIT 29 page 76

Maths
1. 17, 15
2. 8, 7
3. 40, 50, 90
4. 10, 15, 20, 30, 35, 40, 45
5.

6. 10c
7. 3 months
8. Colour the triangle on the left.
9. Parent/teacher to check.
10.

11.

12.

English
1. property
2. polite
3. rules
4. take
5. respect
6. be
7. stare, bare, hare
8. people
9. belongings
10. obey
11. Class rules are important.

UNIT 30 page 78

Maths
1. 18, 12
2. 9, 6
3. 16
4. 80 — twenty
   20 — eighty
   forty — 40
5. Colour 8 ants.
6. Parent/teacher to check.
7. years
8. The see-saw on the left is correct.
9. 2, 3, 1
10.

11.

12. Parent/teacher to check.

English
1. plate
2. eyes
3. paint and decorate
4. mask
5. paint
6. plate
7. thing, ring, king
8. scissors
9. spoon
10. cut, make, paint, attach
11. I can make a paper plate mask.

TEST 4 page 80

Maths
1. 16, 14, 15
2. 9, 10, 11
3. 30, 40, 50, 60, 70, 80, 90
4. seventy, eighty, ninety
5.

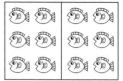

6. 6, 1, 2, 5, 4, 3
7. 9 o'clock
8.

9. shorter
10.

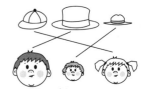

11. △○△○ △○△○
    □△△□ △△□△
    ○○□○ ○○□○○

12. Parent/teacher to check.

English
1. snake
2. smooth
3. school
4. snake
5. silk
6. school
7. Answers will vary: fool, tool, school, pool, rule
8. Answers will vary: bake, take, cake, rake, fake, lake
9. children, people, snakes, days, Dads
10. snake
11. slide, eat, swallow, slither
12. The snake followed Mary to school.

7 MEASUREMENT

Circle the days you
don't go to school.

Monday   Tuesday

Wednesday   Thursday

Friday   Saturday

Sunday

8

Circle the shaded shape which
has the larger area.

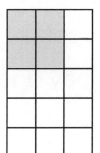 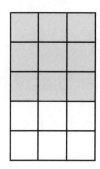

9

Draw a shorter building.

10

Colour the last jug.

11 GEOMETRY

Link.

diamond

circle

        square

        triangle

12

Circle the dinosaur in
the water and colour
the dinosaur under the tree.

Kangaroos are mammals.

A mother kangaroo has a pouch to keep her baby safe.

The baby is a joey and it drinks its mother's milk.

Kangaroos mainly eat grass and leaves.

1 READING & COMPREHENSION

Circle the correct word from the text.

Kangaroos are (cats / dogs / mammals / mothers).

2

Mother kangaroos have (grass / leaves / pouches / mammals).

3

Joeys drink _____ .

4 SPELLING & VOCABULARY **5**

Spell these words from the text.

m i l ___

6

___ o u c h

___ r a s s

7

Make rhyming words.

drink   s _____   s t _____   p _____

it   p _____   h _____   s _____

8

Write the plurals.

kangaroo _____   leaf _____

mammal _____   joey _____

9

GRAMMAR & PUNCTUATION

Link the labels to the picture.   head   mother kangaroo

joey   tail

pouch   legs

10

Circle the adjectives.

hot   cold   mother   kangaroo   grass   green   red

11

Write the sentence correctly.

kangaroos live in australia

_____

Mathematics

NUMBER

1

$$10 + 10 = \boxed{}$$

2

$\boxed{10}$ take away $\boxed{6}$ equals $\boxed{}$

3

Draw 10 fish.

4

Write the words:

12 _____

13 _____

14 _____

5

Draw a line to cut the shapes in half.

6

 + + 20

= $\boxed{}$

MEASUREMENT

7

I would wear these clothes in (spring / summer / autumn / winter).

8

Colour the object with the greatest mass.

9

Circle the widest watch.

10

Colour the last jug.

GEOMETRY

11

Colour the circle which has a line of symmetry.

12

Trace the correct path in red.

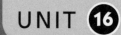

Dad cooked porridge for breakfast this morning. It was nice and warm with milk and honey. I ate it all.

1 READING & COMPREHENSION

Circle the correct word.

Dad cooked (milk / sugar / dinner / porridge).

2 I (like / hate / dislike / spill) porridge.

3 I ate porridge for _____ .

4 SPELLING & VOCABULARY **5**

Spell these words from the text.

___ a d

___ a r m

6 **7**

c ___ ___ k e d

Make rhyming words.

cook   l _____

b _____   t _____

8 Write the plural. one Dad, two _____

9 GRAMMAR & PUNCTUATION

Nouns are naming words. Circle the nouns.

porridge   ate   cooked   milk   honey   Dad

10 Verbs are action words. Complete the sentence with a verb.

Dad _____ breakfast.

11 People's names are proper nouns. Proper nouns need capital letters. Write the sentence correctly.   my sister, lilly, ate porridge too

_____

Mathematics

NUMBER

1

❄❄❄❄❄ + ❄❄
❄❄❄❄❄

10 + 2 = ☐

2

10 frogs. 6 jumped away.
How many are left?

10 take away 6 = ☐

3

How many fish?

☐

4

Write the words.

15 _____

16 _____

17 _____

5

Draw a line to cut each shape into half.

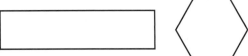

6

Colour the coins you would use to buy the pencil.

MEASUREMENT

7

Colour the winter clothes.

8

Colour the shape with the larger area.

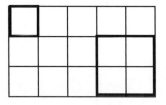

9

Colour the longest object.

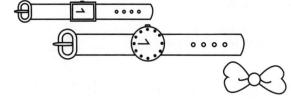

10

Circle the jug which is half full.

GEOMETRY

11

Draw a pattern on the beach towel using these shapes.

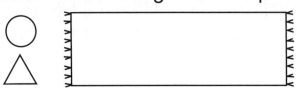

12

Draw a cat to the right of the box.

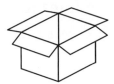

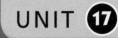

On Sunday my sister and I went to visit
Nanna. Mum took us on the bus.
We stayed all day and had soup for lunch.

1   READING & COMPREHENSION

Circle the correct word.

We went to Nanna's in a (train / bus / car / bike).

2

I visited Nanna on (Sunday / Monday / Friday / yesterday).

3

For lunch we had _____ .

4   SPELLING & VOCABULARY   **5**

Spell these words from the text.

___ u n d a y

s o u ___

6   **7**

d ___ y

Make rhyming words.

day   r _____

p l _____   s t _____

8

Write the plural. one bus, two _____

9   GRAMMAR & PUNCTUATION

Nouns are naming words. Circle the nouns.

sister   went   took   Nanna   Mum

10

Verbs are action words. Complete the sentence with a verb.

We _____ soup for lunch.

11

Names of days and people are proper nouns. Proper nouns need
capital letters. Write the sentence correctly.

on sunday i went to visit nanna _____

Mathematics

1

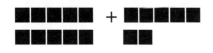

10 + 7 = ☐

2

8 take away 5 equals ☐

3

_____ , 2, 3, 4, 5, _____

4

Write the numerals.

eighteen _____

nineteen _____

5

Colour one half of each shape.

6

Circle the right money to buy the bear.

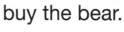  

7

 _____ o'clock

8

Draw a shape that covers 5 squares.

9

Colour the deepest container.

10

Circle the teddy which will fit into the box.

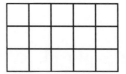

11

Link the matching patterns.

12

Help the child get home.

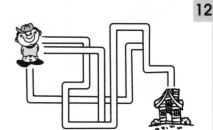

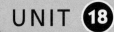
Yesterday the children in 1K went on a visit to the park. We played on the slide and had a picnic lunch.

1 READING & COMPREHENSION

Circle the correct word.

The children went to the (lunch / shop / school / park).

2 1K went on the visit (Sunday / today / yesterday / Monday).

3 The children had a picnic _____ .

4 SPELLING & VOCABULARY **5**

Spell these words from the text.

___ ___ i l d r e n

l u n ___ ___

6

p ___ c n ___ c

7 Make rhyming words.

lunch   p _____

m _____   c r _____

8 Write the plural. one lunch, ten _____

9 GRAMMAR & PUNCTUATION

Nouns are naming words. Choose a noun from the box that matches the group.
breakfast, dinner, _____

food
lunch
soup

10 Verbs are action words. Choose a verb from the list.

The children _____ on the slide.

drove, swam, played, chewed

11 A sentence begins with a capital letter and ends in a full stop.
Write the sentence correctly.   the children had a picnic lunch

_____

Mathematics

1
NUMBER

XXXXX + XXXXXX
XXXXX   XXX

10 + 8 = ☐

2

| 20 | take away | 10 | equals | ☐ |

3

How many apples are on the tree?

☐

4

Write the words.

18 _____

19 _____

20 _____

5

Colour one half of each shape.

6

Choose the right money. Tick it.

7
MEASUREMENT

Colour the picture which shows spring.

8

Circle the object with the greatest mass.

9

Draw something that is as tall as you.

10

Colour the mouse that will fit in the hole.

11
GEOMETRY

Continue the patterns.

 ___ ___ ___

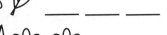 ___ ___ ___

12

Circle the apple on the left of the pineapple.

52

Dear Tooth Fairy,
Please take my tooth. It fell out today when I ate a carrot.   Love Tran

1 READING & COMPREHENSION

Circle the correct word.

The tooth fell out (yesterday / tomorrow / today / when).

2 Tran was eating a (carrot / apple / orange / fairy).

3 Whose tooth fell out? _____ tooth fell out.

4 SPELLING & VOCABULARY **5**

Spell these words from the text.

___ e a r

w h e ___

6 **7**

t ___ ___ t h

Make rhyming words.

take   b _____

c _____   s h _____

8

Write the plural. one baby, some_____

9 GRAMMAR & PUNCTUATION

Nouns are naming words. Circle the nouns.

tooth   carrot   fairy   fell   take   please

10 Verbs are action words. Complete the sentence with a verb.

Tran's tooth _____ out.

11 A sentence begins with a capital letter and ends in a full stop. Names start with capital letters. Write the sentence correctly.

tran wrote to the tooth fairy _____

Mathematics

NUMBER

1

 +  = ☐

8 + 5 = ☐

2

20 take away 6 equals ☐

3

10 sharks and 2 sharks.
How many sharks?

☐

4

Write the numerals

eighteen _____   nineteen _____

twenty _____

5

Colour one half of
the bananas.

6

Colour the 50 cent pieces
which make one dollar.

MEASUREMENT

7

What day is today?

_____

8

The apple is
(heavier / lighter) than the cherries.

9

Draw something that is
as long as your arm.

10

Colour the last jug.

GEOMETRY

11

Continue the pattern.

    __ __ __

12

Help the
mouse
to its hole.

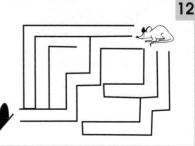

The lion caught a mouse. The mouse begged the lion not to eat it and promised to repay the kindness one day. When the lion got caught in a net the mouse ate through the ropes. The lion was free.

1   READING & COMPREHENSION

Circle the correct word.

The lion caught a (rope / net / mouse / house).

2   The mouse ate the (lion / ropes / tiger / tree).

3   The lion was _____ .

4   SPELLING & VOCABULARY   **5**

Spell these words from the text.

_____ i o n

n e _____

6   **7**

r _____ p e

Make rhyming words.

eat   b _____

m _____   t r _____

8

Write the plural. one mouse, ten _____

9   GRAMMAR & PUNCTUATION

Nouns are naming words. Choose a noun from the box which matches the group.

lion, leopard, _____

dog
tiger
mouse

10   Verbs are action words. Complete the sentence with a verb.

The mouse _____ through the net.

11   A sentence begins with a capital letter and ends in a full stop. Write the sentence correctly. the mouse repaid the lion's kindness

_____

Mathematics

NUMBER

1

⊛⊛⊛⊛⊛ + ⊛⊛⊛⊛⊛
⊛⊛⊛⊛ ⊛⊛⊛⊛

9 + 9 = ☐

2

☐ – 4 equals ☐

3

10 and 3 flowers.

How many flowers?

☐

4

Count by 5s.

5, 10, ____, ____, ____, ____,

____, ____, ____, ____

5

Draw a line to cut each shape in half.

6

Colour the money needed to buy two apples. 50c

7

Colour the clothes to wear in summer.

MEASUREMENT

8

Draw a shape that covers 6 squares.

9

Draw something that is as wide as your hand.

10

Which house takes up more space?

GEOMETRY

11

Use these shapes to draw a face.

12

A _____ is on the left of the flower.

The hare said, "I am faster than you, tortoise. I will race you." The hare went to sleep and the tortoise won the race.

1

Circle the correct word.

The race was won by the (hare / tortoise / turtle / faster).

2 The hare went to (bed / dinner / sleep / rest).

3 The hare and the tortoise had a _____ .

---

4   **5**

Spell these words from the text.

___ a r e

w o ___

6 **7**

r ___ c e

Make rhyming words.

hare   s h _____

f _____ d _____

8 Write the plural. one race, two _____

9

Nouns are naming words. Choose a noun from the box.

Who won the race? The _____

pig, rabbit, hare, tortoise

10 Verbs are action words. Choose a verb from the list.

The tortoise _____ the hare.

ate, raced, drove, jumped

11 A sentence begins with a capital letter and ends in a full stop.
Write the sentence correctly. slow and steady wins the race

_____

NUMBER

1

☆☆☆☆☆☆ + ☆☆☆
☆☆☆☆☆☆

12 + 3 = ☐

2

☒ ☒ ☒ ☒ ☒
✂ ✂ ✂ ✂ ✂

☐ – ☐ = ☐

3

____ and ____ dogs

= ☐ 15 ☐ dogs

4

Link:　　10　　　　　ten

　　　　20　　　　　thirty

　　　　30　　　　　twenty

5

Colour half of
the strawberries.

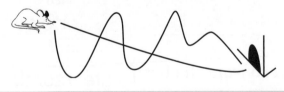

6

How many make $1.00?
Cross out the extra coins.

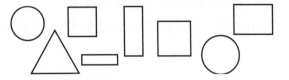

MEASUREMENT

7

Draw what you had
for breakfast today.

8

Which is heavier,
10 spoons or 6 spoons?

____ spoons are heavier than

____ spoons.

9

Trace the shorter path
home for the mouse.

10

Draw a jug that
is half empty.

GEOMETRY

11

Colour the circles and
draw stripes on the squares.

12

Colour the koala
beside the tree.

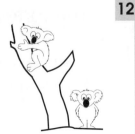

Birds have feathers and wings and two legs.
Most birds can fly but some birds cannot fly. The
emu is a bird that cannot fly but it can run very fast.

1   READING & COMPREHENSION

Circle the correct word.

Birds have two (legs / heads / feathers / eggs).

2   Most birds can (drive / fly / jump / hop).

3   The emu cannot _____ .

4   SPELLING & VOCABULARY   **5**

Spell these words from the text.

___ e r y

b i r ___

6

f l ___

7

Make rhyming words.

fly   s p _____

d r _____   c r _____

8

Write the plural. one bird, a flock of _____

9   GRAMMAR & PUNCTUATION

Nouns are naming words. Circle the nouns.

bird   fast   emu   eggs   fly

10   Verbs are action words. Circle the verbs that describe what birds do.

fly   walk   eat   emu   fast   two

11   A sentence begins with a capital letter and ends in a full stop. Write the sentence correctly. emus are australian birds that cannot fly

_____

Mathematics

1

NUMBER

$12 + 3 =$ ▢

2

▢ – ▢ = ▢

3

10 and 6 clowns =

▢ clowns

4

Write the numerals.

forty _____   sixty _____

fifty _____   seventy _____

5

Draw a line of symmetry and colour half the clown.

6

Colour how many make $1.00.

7

MEASUREMENT

The time is

_____ o'clock.

8

The _____ is heavier.

9

How many pencil lengths long is your desk? Guess, then measure.

Guess _____   Measure _____

10

Colour the last jug.

11

GEOMETRY

Draw spots on the triangles.

12

Trace a path on the lines for the dog to get home.

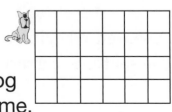

Some children walk to school. Some children are driven to school in cars. Other children come to school on the bus. Some children have school at home.

How do you get to school?

1   READING & COMPREHENSION

Circle the correct word.

Some children (walk / fly / swim / float) to school.

2   Some children come to school by (spaceship / car / helicopter / mouse).

3   Some children have school at _____ .

4   SPELLING & VOCABULARY   **5**

Spell these words from the text.

___ a l k

s c h o o ___

6   **7**

s c h ___ ___ l

Make rhyming words.

drive   h _____

f _____   d _____

8   Write the plural. one child, many _____

9   GRAMMAR & PUNCTUATION

Nouns are naming words. Choose a noun from the box which matches the group.

car, bus, _____

| lion |
| school |
| train |

10   Verbs are action words. Answer the question with a verb.

How do you get to school? _____

11   A sentence begins with a capital letter and ends in a full stop. Write the sentence correctly. most children at our school come

by car _____

1   NUMBER   **2**

8   +   4   =

10   +   2   =

20 – 5 =

20 – 8 =

3

10 and 5 lollies

=

4

Link:

17   20

eighteen   nineteen

19   18

twenty   seventeen

5

Colour half the butterflies.

6

Colour any coins to make $1.00.

7

Show what time
you go to bed.

8

The (apple / pineapple)
is heavier.

9

Trace the shorter
path home for the dog.

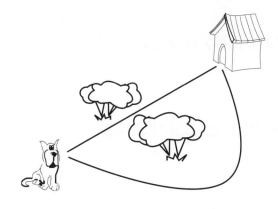

10

Colour the flowers
which suit the vase.

11

Colour the triangles red
and the rectangles green.

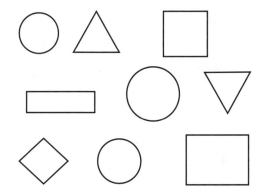

12

The beetle is
(on / under) the leaf.

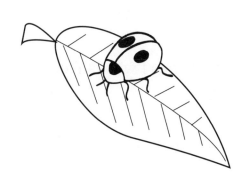

Goldilocks went into the bears' house.
She ate some porridge, broke a chair
and then she went to sleep on the bed.
When the three bears came home
they found her in bed.
She screamed and ran away.

---

1 READING & COMPREHENSION

Circle the correct word from the text.

Goldilocks ate (toast / bears / porridge / honey).

2

When the bears came home they found Goldilocks
in a (chair / bed / eating / running away).

3

Goldilocks broke a _____ .

---

4 SPELLING & VOCABULARY **5**

Spell these words from
the text.

c h a i ____

6

____ e n t

b ___ ___ r

7

Make rhyming words.

bed　r _____　　　l _____　　　T _____

sleep　p _____　　　s h _____　　　s t _____

8

Write the plurals.

house _____　　　chair _____

bear _____　　　bed _____

9

GRAMMAR & PUNCTUATION

Circle the nouns.

bear　　ate　　Goldilocks　　bed　　chair　　sleep

10

Answer the question with a sentence.

What did Goldilocks do when she saw the bears?

_____

_____

11

Write the sentence correctly.

goldilocks went into the house

_____

1

NUMBER

✓✓✓✓✓
✓✓✓✓✓ + ☐ = 20
✓✓✓✓✓

15 + ☐ = 20

2

☐ − ☐ = ☐

3

Count by 5s.

_____, 10, _____, 20, _____,

30, _____, 40, _____, 50

4

Write the words.

40 _____

50 _____

60 _____

5

Colour half the flowers red
and half blue.

6

 + + +

= ☐

7

MEASUREMENT

The time is

_____ o'clock.

8

The _____
is lighter.

9

Use pencils to measure
the length of your TV.

My TV is _____ pencils long.

10

Draw a container that will
hold less than the jug.

11

GEOMETRY

Draw a pattern
on the squares.

12

Draw a cloud
above the
plane and a
smaller cloud
below the plane.

Hermit crabs make interesting pets. They are very clean. They don't eat very much and they are quite friendly if you train them. They like to swap shells quite often so they need empty shells in their tank.

1   READING & COMPREHENSION

Circle the correct word.

Hermit crabs are (good / bad / silly / greedy) pets.

2

Hermit crabs are not (clean / dirty / happy / interesting).

3

Hermit crabs are _____ .

4   SPELLING & VOCABULARY   **5**

Spell these words from the text.

___ l e a n

c r a ___

6   **7**

q u ___ t e

Make rhyming words.

clean   m _____

b _____   l _____

8

Write the plural. one crab, two _____

9   GRAMMAR & PUNCTUATION

Nouns are naming words.

Link the labels to the crab.

shell

eye

leg

10

Verbs are action words. Circle the verbs that describe what crabs do.

eat   friendly   pet   run   crawl   move

11

Write the sentence correctly.
hermit crabs eat coconut, bread, biscuits and fish food

_____

Mathematics

NUMBER

1

$$18 + \boxed{} = 20$$

2

$$\boxed{20} - \boxed{8} = \boxed{}$$

3

Give the hen 15 chicks.

4

Write the numerals.

seventy _____ eighty _____

ninety _____

5

Circle the shapes that are cut in half.

6

 +  +

= ☐

7

MEASUREMENT

What time is it?

_____ o'clock

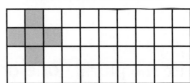

8

Draw a shape with the same area.

9

How many pencils long is your bed?

Guess _____   Measure _____

10

Draw a container and show half full.

11

Continue the patterns.

GEOMETRY

12

Draw a boat behind the car.

Dinosaurs lived long ago. Dinosaurs are extinct now. Scientists dig up dinosaur fossils and study them for clues to how dinosaurs lived. Some dinosaurs were meat-eaters and some dinosaurs ate plants.

1   READING & COMPREHENSION

Circle the correct word.

Scientists study dinosaur (food / fossils / clues / meat).

2   Some dinosaurs ate (fossils / meat / scientists / dirt).

3   Dinosaurs are now _____ .

4   SPELLING & VOCABULARY   **5**

Spell these words from the text.

___ i n o s a u r

f o s s i ___

6   **7**

Make rhyming words.

s t u d ___

meat   h _____

t r _____   s _____

8   Write the plural. **one dinosaur,** no _____

9   GRAMMAR & PUNCTUATION

Nouns are naming words.

Link the labels to the dinosaur.

eyes

head

mouth

body

10   Verbs are action words. Circle the verbs that describe what dinosaurs do.

run   eat   old   talk   scratch   big

11   A sentence begins with a capital letter and ends in a full stop. Write the sentence correctly.

dinosaurs are extinct _____

Mathematics

NUMBER

1

☆ ☆ ☆ ☆ ☆ ☆ ☆ ☆
☆ ☆ ☆ ☆ ☆ ☆ ☆ ☆

8 + ☐ = 20

2

20 − 4 = ☐

3

Draw 11 kittens for
the mother cat.

4

Link: 70   seventy

80   ninety

90   eighty

5

Colour half of the balloons.

6

Colour how many coins
make 50c.

MEASUREMENT

7

The time is

_____ o'clock.

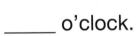

8

Draw a shape that
covers 8 squares.

9

How many giant steps
long is your room?

Guess _____   Measure _____

10

Circle which containers
will hold sand.

GEOMETRY

11

Continue the pattern.

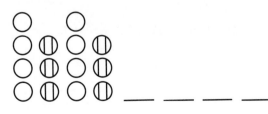
__ __ __ __

12

Draw a dog on the
left of the child.

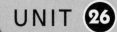
Whales and dolphins are mammals. The mothers feed their young milk. Whales and dolphins are very smart. They live in groups called pods.

---

1 READING & COMPREHENSION

Circle the correct word.

Whales are (dolphins / mammals / fish / sharks).

---

2 Whales live in groups called (pods / young / mammals / dolphins).

---

3 Mammal mothers feed their babies _____ .

---

4 SPELLING & VOCABULARY **5**

Spell these words from the text.

___ o u n g

m a m m a ___

---

6 **7**

w h ___ l e

Make rhyming words.

whale   p _____

m _____   s _____

8

Write the plural. one mother, many _____

---

9 GRAMMAR & PUNCTUATION

Nouns are naming words. Choose a noun from the box.

Whales and dolphins are _____ .

mammals, fish, birds, reptiles

---

10 Verbs are action words. Complete the sentence with a verb.

Mammals _____ their babies milk.

---

11 A sentence begins with a capital letter and ends in a full stop.
Write the sentence correctly.   i love whales and dolphins

_____

Mathematics

NUMBER

1

$7 +$ ☐ $= 20$

$5 +$ ☐ $= 20$

○○○○○○○○○○○○○○○○○○○○

2

$20 - 5 =$ ☐

$20 - 6 =$ ☐

○○○○○○○○○○○○○○○○○○○○

3 Circle which row has the most flowers.

❀ ❀ ❀ ❀ ❀ ❀ ❀ ❀ ❀ ❀

❀ ❀ ❀ ❀ ❀ ❀ ❀ ❀ ❀ ❀

4 Write the numerals.

one hundred _____

ninety _____   eighty _____

5 Colour one half of the apples.

6 Number the money in order of value.

____   ____   ____   ____

MEASUREMENT

7

The time is

_____ o'clock.

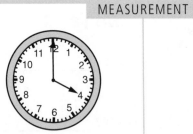

8 Draw a shape that covers 7 squares.

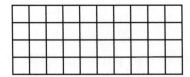

9 How many foot lengths long is your room?

Guess _____   Measure _____

10 Which one will hold the most sand? Circle it.

GEOMETRY

11 Draw circles to make the pattern.

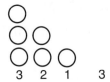

3 2 1   3 2 1   3 2 1

12 Draw a bird on the girl's right side and a cat on her left side.

English

Television wasn't invented when my grandfather was a boy. His family listened to the radio every night.

1

Circle the correct word.

The family listened to the radio every (month / week / night).

2 Television wasn't invented (now / then / when / soon).

3 Grandfather listened to the _____ .

4 **5**

Spell these words from the text.

b ___ y

w h ___ n

6   **7**

w ___ s

Make rhyming words.

night   r _____

s _____   f r _____

8

Write the plural. one family, seven _____

9

Adjectives are describing words. Choose an adjective from the box.

Television is a _____ invention.

> wet
> sad
> terrific

10 Choose a verb from the box. Complete the sentence.

"Turn the television off!" _____ Mum.

> whispered,
> yelled, cheeped

11 Commands tell someone to do something. Write the command.
Use an exclamation mark (!).   turn it off

_____

Mathematics

1

$$2 + \boxed{} = 20$$

$$\boxed{} + 2 = 20$$

OOOOOOOOOOOOOOOOOOOO

2

$$15 - 5 = \boxed{}$$

$$15 - 10 = \boxed{}$$

OOOOOOOOOOOOOOOOOOOOOO

3

Join the dots.

4

Link.   100   ninety

          90   one hundred

          80   eighty

5

Draw the matching half.

6

Circle the most valuable.

7

The time is

_____ o'clock.

8

Draw something that has nearly the same mass as you.

9

How many body lengths long is your room?

Guess _____   Measure _____

10

Match the rings to the fingers.

11

Draw an object that has this shape.

12

Draw an orange on the left of the knife.

74

How to look after your teeth

1.   Brush your teeth after meals.
2.   Floss your teeth every day.
3.   Eat food rich in calcium.

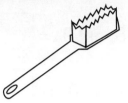

1   READING & COMPREHENSION

Circle the correct word.

Look after your (socks / soup / teeth / feet).

2   Floss your teeth every (week / year / day / hour).

3   Teeth need food rich in _____ .

4   SPELLING & VOCABULARY   **5**

Spell these words from the text.

___ o o d

t e e ___ ___

6   **7**

h ___ ___

Make rhyming words.

how   c _____

n _____   s _____

8   Write the plural.   one tooth,   many _____

9   GRAMMAR & PUNCTUATION

Nouns are naming words.   Circle the nouns.

yoghurt   milk   eat   clean   apples   cheese

10   A command often begins with a verb.   Complete the command with a verb.

_____ your teeth after meals.

11   This sentence is a command. Write the sentence correctly.
brush your teeth before you go to bed

_____

Mathematics

1

$$8 + 9 = \boxed{}$$

$$7 + 8 = \boxed{}$$

2

$$16 - 8 = \boxed{}$$

$$14 - 7 = \boxed{}$$

OOOOOOOOOOOOOOOOOOOOO

3

Write the missing numbers.

10, 20, 30, _____ , _____ ,

60, 70, 80, _____ , 100

4

Write the missing numbers on the number line.

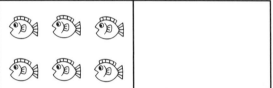

0 5   25   50

5

Draw the matching half.

6

Circle the least valuable.

7

Circle the correct answer.

Winter lasts for

(two / three / four) months.

8

Colour the shape which has the greater area.

9

Draw a longer shoe.

10

Match the dog to its kennel.

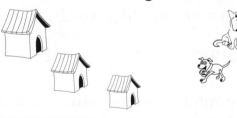

11

Continue the patterns.

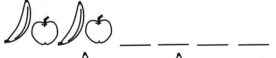

12

Draw a hat on the child in the middle.

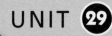

Class Rules
1. Be polite.
2. Take care of your property.
3. Respect other people's feelings and property.

1 READING & COMPREHENSION

Circle the correct word.

Take care of your (property / friends / lunch / Nanna).

2 Be (cranky / sad / hungry / polite).

3 We must obey the class _____ .

4 SPELLING & VOCABULARY **5**

Spell these words from the text.

___ a k e

r e s p e c ___

6 **7**

b ___

Make rhyming words.

care   st _____

b _____   h _____

8

Write the plural. one person, two _____

9 GRAMMAR & PUNCTUATION

Nouns are naming words. Choose a noun from the box that means 'property'. _____

belongings
people
rules

10

Verbs are action words. Choose a verb from the list.

_____ the class rules.

Take, Skip,
Make, Obey

11

A sentence begins with a capital letter and ends in a full stop.
Write the sentence correctly.   class rules are important

_____

1   NUMBER

$$9 + 9 = \boxed{}$$

$$6 + 6 = \boxed{}$$

2

$$18 - 9 = \boxed{}$$

$$12 - 6 = \boxed{}$$

3

How many pies? $\boxed{}$

4

Link.   80   twenty

         20   eighty

    forty   40

5

Colour half of the ants.

6

Colour coins to make one dollar.

7   MEASUREMENT

Growing up takes

(days / weeks / months / years).

8

Circle the correct one.

9

Number the objects
in order from shortest to longest.

10

Match the present to its box.

11   GEOMETRY

Draw circles to
make the pattern.

4   2   4   2   1   4   2   4   2   1

12

Help Lilly
get to
the shop.

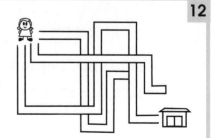

How to make a mask
1.   Cut two eye holes in a paper plate.
2.   Paint and decorate the plate.
3.   Attach strings to the side of the plate.

1   READING & COMPREHENSION
Circle the correct word.

You can make a mask with a (cup / plate / fork / hole).

2   To see through the mask you need to cut (ears / eyes / hair / a mouth).

3   You can _____ and _____ the plate.

4   SPELLING & VOCABULARY   **5**
Spell these words from the text.

___ a s k

p a i n ___

6   **7**

p l ___ t e

Make rhyming words.

string   t h _____

r _____   k _____

8   Write the plural.
one pair of scissors, two pairs of _____

9   GRAMMAR & PUNCTUATION
Nouns are naming words. Choose a noun from the box which matches the group.

plate, fork, _____

lion
spoon
mask

10   Circle the verbs which describe what you do to make a paper plate mask.

cut   paper   make   paint   string   eye   attach

11   A sentence begins with a capital letter and ends in a full stop.
Write the sentence correctly.   i can make a paper plate mask

_____

Mathematics

NUMBER

1

9 + 7 = ☐

8 + 6 = ☐

7 + 8 = ☐

2

17 – 8 = ☐

19 – 9 = ☐

18 – 7 = ☐

3

Write the missing numbers.

10, 20, ____ , ____ ,

____ , ____ , ____ ,

____ , ____ , 100

4

Write the words.

70 _____

80 _____

90 _____

5

Draw the matching half.

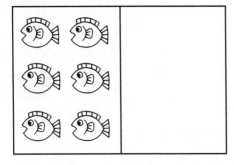

6

Number the coins in order of value from least to most.

____ ____ ____

____ ____ ____

Mathematics

MEASUREMENT

7

The time is _____ o'clock.

8

Circle the closed shapes.

9

The belt is (longer / shorter) than the scarf.

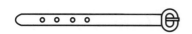

10

Match the person to the hats.

GEOMETRY

11

Continue the patterns.

△○△○__ __ __ __

▢△△▢__ __ __ __

○○▢○○__ __ __ __

12

Help Ben get home from school.
Trace the shortest path.

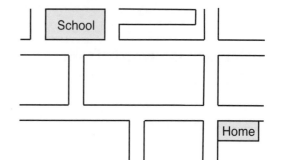

Mary had a little snake,
little snake, little snake.
Mary had a little snake
Its skin was smooth as silk.

It followed her to school one day,
school one day, school one day.
It followed her to school one day
Which was against the rules.

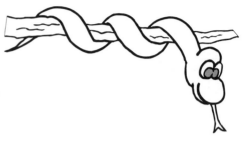

---

1   READING & COMPREHENSION

Circle the correct word from the text.

Mary had a (silk / snake / school / yell).

2

The snake's skin was (cool / little / smooth / skin).

3

The snake followed Mary to _____ .

---

4   SPELLING & VOCABULARY   **5**

Spell these words from
the text.

s ____ l k

6

____ n a k e

s c h o o ____

7

Make rhyming words.

cool _____ _____ _____

snake _____ _____ _____

8

Write the plurals. snake _____

child _____ day _____

person _____ Dad _____

9

Choose a noun from the box.

lamb, run, school, snake, slither

Mary had a _____ .

10

Circle the verbs which describe what a snake can do.

slide   eat   jump   yell   swallow   slither   hop

11

Write the sentence correctly.

the snake followed mary to school

_____

© 1999 Tanya Dalgleish and Pascal Press
Reprinted 2000, 2001 (twice), 2005, 2006, 2007, 2008 (twice), 2009, 2010, 2011 (twice)

Updated in 2013 for the Australian Curriculum

Reprinted 2014 (twice), 2016, 2017, 2018, 2019, 2020 (twice), 2021

ISBN 978 1 86441 336 6

Pascal Press
PO Box 250
Glebe NSW 2037
(02) 858 4044
www.pascalpress.com.au

Publisher: Vivienne Joannou
Australian Curriculum updates edited by Rosemary Peers and
    answers checked by Peter Little
Typeset by Precision Typesetting (Barbara Nilsson)
    and lj Design (Julianne Billington)
Cover by DiZign Pty Ltd
Printed by Vivar Printing/Green Giant Press